# GENOMICS
## and Cloning

SANDY FRITZ

A+

## PHOTO CREDITS

Pages 4, 7, 30: Copyright © 2003 Hemera Technologies Inc. All rights reserved. Page 5: TIME LIFE PICTURES. Pages 6, 8, 15, 16, 19: Courtesy U.S. Department of Energy Human Genome Program, http://www.ornl.gov/hgmis. Page 9: Dr. Nelson Max, University of California, Lawrence Livermore Laboratory and the Department of Energy. Pages 10-11: Courtesy National Human Genome Research Institute. Page 18: Geoffrey Stewart/Hybrid Medical Animation. Page 22: M. Steven Doggett. Page 23: sickle.bwh.edu/thal_inheritance.html. Art: Joe Bailey. Page 24: CDC. Page 26: Omikron/Photo Researchers. Page 28 (top to bottom): Copyright © 2003 Bill Love, Michael Tweedie/Photo Researchers. Page 31: Copyright © 2003 Wim van Egmond. Page 33:Roselin Institute. Pages 34, 38: Courtesy Paul Berg. Page 35: Andrew Martinez/Photo Researchers. Page 36: Art copyright © 2003 Phil Wilson. Page 37: Andrew Leonard/Photo Researchers. Page 38: Artwork originally created for the National Cancer Institute. Reprinted with permission of the artist, Jeanne Kelly. Copyright © 1996. Page 39 (Left to right): Courtesy U.S. Department of Energy Human Genome Program, http://www.ornl.gov/hgmis, Science Photo Library/Photo Researchers. Page 40: Geoffrey Stewart/Hybrid Medical Animation. Page 42: Eye of Science2/Photo Researchers. Pages 43, 44: Art copyright © 2003 Karen Carr.

Published by Smart Apple Media
1980 Lookout Drive, North Mankato, Minnesota 56003

Produced by Byron Preiss Visual Publications, Inc.
Copyright © 2003 Byron Preiss Visual Publications

Edited by Howard Zimmerman
Associate editor: Janine Rosado
Graphics editor: Robin Bader
Design templates by Tom Draper Studio
Cover and interior layouts by Gilda Hannah
Cover art: copyright © 2003 the van Heesch brothers (http://www.stack.nl/~fidget)

Library of Congress Cataloging-in-Publication Data

Fritz, Sandy.
Genomics and cloning / by Sandy Fritz.
p. cm. — (Hot science)
Summary: A discussion of the field of genetics, focusing on the study of the human genome, genetic engineering, and cloning.

ISBN 1-58340-365-5

1. Genomics—Juvenile literature. 2. Genetic engineering—Juvenile literature. 3. Cloning—Juvenile literature. [1. Genetics. 2. Genetic engineering. 3. Cloning.] I. Title. II. Series.
QH437.5.F75 2003          572.8'6—dc21          2003042751

First Edition

9 8 7 6 5 4 3 2 1

# CONTENTS

## New Old Science

# INTRODUCTION

Advances in genetic engineering and cloning are making news headlines around the world. To many, it may seem as though these are new sciences, but both have long histories. For thousands of years, people have been genetically engineering animals—without knowing it. When an animal appeared among an ancient tribe's herds that had desired qualities, the tribe would breed that animal with another of a similar nature. Slowly, sometimes over centuries, the qualities people didn't like in that species of animal vanished, and the properties they did like became firmly established. This type of genetic engineering is called "selective breeding." This is how the quick, long-legged, intelligent mountain sheep became the fat, short-legged, and slow-witted sheep ranchers have today.

Ancient people extended the same selective breeding methods to the crops they grew. Plants with qualities desired by people were nurtured, and their seeds used to sow the next year's crop. Plants that were not what people wanted were pulled out of the ground and destroyed. Thanks to this kind of selective breeding, wild grasses became fields of rice, wheat, and barley. Many of the foods we enjoy today, including corn, squash, tomatoes, potatoes, and peanuts, were developed by selective breeding in early societies.

These genetic engineering pioneers didn't understand the dynamics behind

**Dumbed-down and fattened-up, today's sheep are the product of centuries of selective breeding by ranchers.**

what they were doing, but they understood that it worked. It wasn't until the end of the 19th century that an Austrian monk named Gregor Mendel began to describe the biology of genetics. Mendel carefully bred pea plants and began to identify what he called "atoms of inheritance" that governed what a pea plant would look like. Today, we recognize that Mendel's atoms of inheritance are "genes."

Understanding genes and the genome and genetic engineering and cloning does take a certain amount of effort. But once the basic principles are understood, the key to life on Earth appears. Everything human beings identify as a living creature is made of cells. Some creatures are made of just one cell. Some are made of trillions of cells. Although all cells are not the same, similar principles and parts guide their development.

The same patterns, even the same substances, are found in all living things. Slight variations in the organization of these substances and components give rise to the great diversity of plants and animals on the planet.

A portrait of Gregor Mendel, who pioneered the science of plant genetics more than 100 years ago.

Understanding the basic nature of cells leads to a new sense of wonder about the world. It leads us to ponder the nature of ourselves and of all living things. In the end, the exploration of the human genome has led us to understand that the processes underpinning all living things are quite similar, no matter how different living things appear to be.

# The Book of Life

## CHAPTER ONE

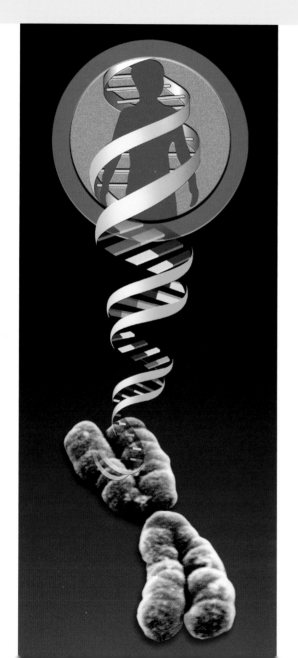

The logo of the U.S. Human Genome Project, which is a joint effort between the Department of Energy and the National Institutes of Health. It features a strand of DNA uncoiling from a chromosome at the bottom.

Within nearly every cell in the human body lies a map. Every teardrop, every skin cell washed down the drain, even a mere touch that leaves behind trace moisture, contains an entire map of a person. The codes for the shape of your bones, the color of your eyes, and the size of your feet are embedded in the nearly 10 trillion cells that make up your body. Each of your cells carries the blueprint that defines what a human being is. And, along with that general plan, each cell also carries the information for making one unique human being—*you*.

Thousands upon thousands of "invisible actions" take place in the human body that keep you alive. Humans must breathe air. The oxygen in air must be removed. Then the oxygen must be carried to all parts of the body to help keep cells alive. The liver cleanses the blood. The stomach adds acids to the food we eat to break it down. Nerve cells are like highways connecting all the different organs in the body. Each internal organ has a lifetime's worth of work to do. We do not consciously direct this work. It is something a healthy body does by itself without any thought from us.

The blueprint of life that directs these miraculous systems is found in the human genome. The genome defines and maintains the physical traits of the human family. It provides the instructions that tell cells how to direct the physical and chemical functions of life.

The human genome contains the map that directs the general traits that are common to all human beings. Most people have one head, two hands, two feet, etc. These characteristics are common to the human family. Yet some people have black hair and some people have blonde hair. Some people have long fingers and some have short fingers. These differences between people are caused by tiny variations in structures called "genes." Variations in genes make each person unique. Nearly every single cell in your body carries not just the genes it needs for its job, but your entire genome as well. So the genome directs the general traits that appear in all people, while slight variations in genes allow for the traits that make you unique in the world. Fingerprints are common to every person, yet every person's fingerprints are unique. In the same way, the human genome is common to all people, but the genome inside your cells is unique to you.

Every fingerprint on every person ever born is unique to that person. That's why fingerprints are used by law enforcement agencies to identify suspected criminals.

Genomes are not unique to human beings. All living creatures have their own genomes. Each species of fish, every type of tree, even bacteria have their own individual genomes. Although a mouse and a human being seem to have little in common, as much as 99 percent of the mouse genome contains the same genes as

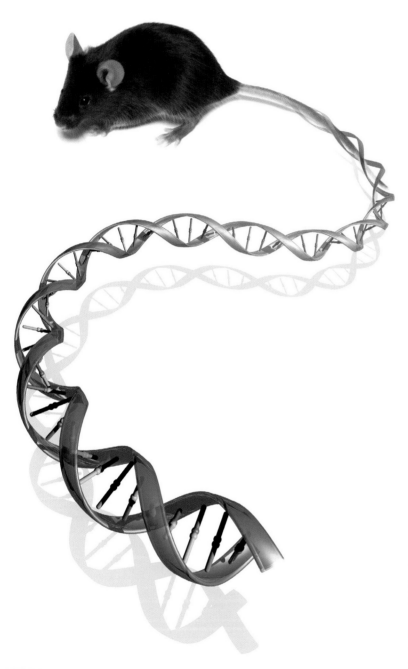

the human genome. The physical and chemical processes that define what a mouse is are quite similar to the physical and chemical processes that define a human being.

The presence of a genome in all living things, and the similarities of their structures, suggests that all earthly life is united and may have sprung from a common source. In fact, the genes that give rise to a mouse, a fish, or a bacterium—or to any other living creature—are all made from the exact same chemical substance. This substance is a molecule called deoxyribonucleic acid, or "DNA."

One hundred years ago, few people would have accepted the idea that a molecule could carry the entire set of operating instructions for a living organism. And yet, the DNA molecule does just that. It was discovered deep inside the nucleus of cells on tiny structures called "chromosomes." Scientists knew chromosomes were involved in

Left: The humble mouse was the first mammal to have its genome decoded, as represented by this computer-generated illustration.

Opposite page: This illustration shows the incredibly complex twisting and coiling a **DNA** molecule must undergo in order to fit into the nucleus of a cell.

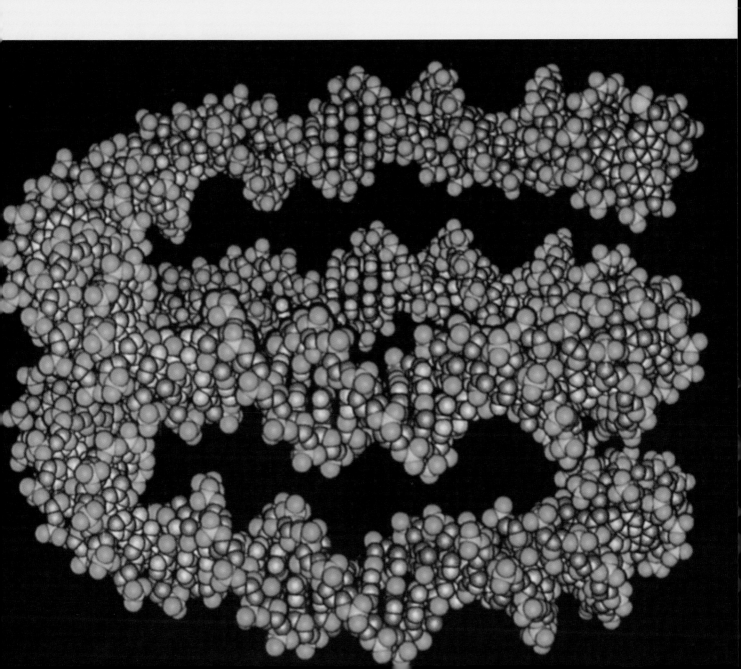

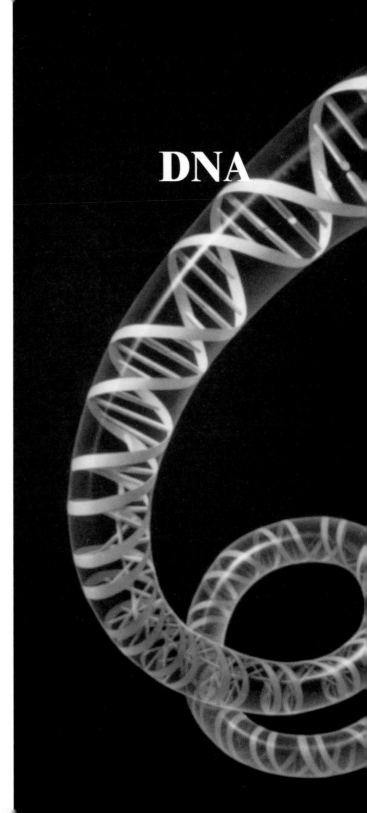

the functioning of cells. But it took them a long time to understand how DNA works.

Chromosomes are tiny, threadlike structures that lie at the heart of a cell, in its nucleus. Chromosomes are made mostly of DNA. When unraveled, the structure of DNA is revealed to be composed mostly of genes. Genes, in turn, are sequences of molecules called "nucleotides." DNA, genes, and nucleotides are all parts of the genome. These basic parts, along with some others, make up the whole.

One way to understand the whole of the human genome, and its parts, is to think of it as a book. A book is bound in a cover, has lots of pages, and is broken up into chapters. The chapters of a book are composed of paragraphs, and the paragraphs themselves are composed of words. The words, in turn, are made up of letters. Every cell in the human body, with the exception of red blood cells and cells related to reproduction, carries a full copy of the entire book. This "book" is the human genome.

Books need a cover and a spine to keep the pages organized. In the human genome,

**DNA is located in chromosomes, which are found in the nucleus of a cell.**

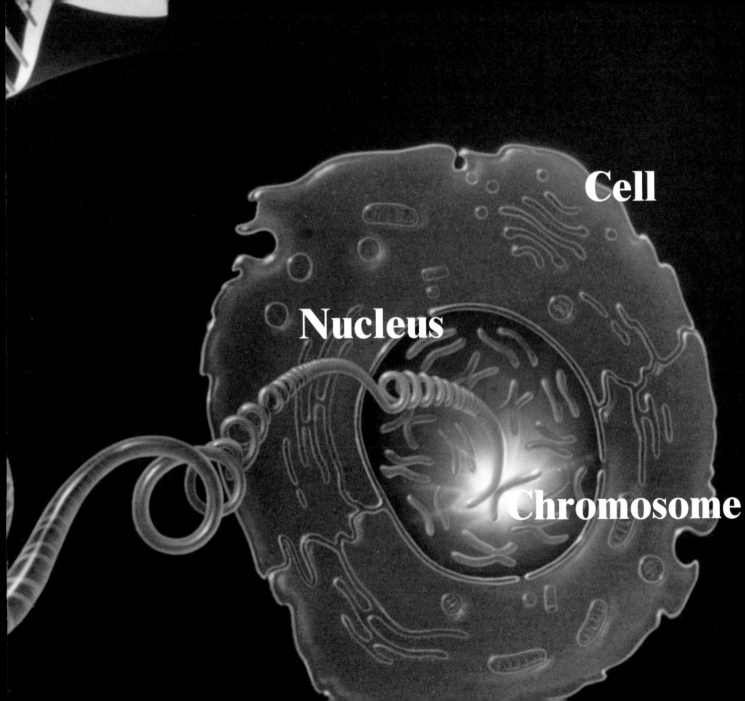

Red blood cells have no nucleus. This means they have no DNA. Why does nearly every cell in the body get a full set of DNA and red blood cells get left behind? Red blood cells have one key job. They circulate through the body, bringing cells oxygen and taking away carbon dioxide ($CO_2$). To do this they need to be able to squeeze into some pretty tight places. Lacking a nucleus gives blood cells the flexibility to fold into tiny areas so they can perform their oxygen delivery and $CO_2$ removal responsibilities. Besides red blood cells, which carry no genetic instructions, the sperm and egg cell involved in reproduction are the only cells in the human body that do not include a full copy of the genome.

the spine and the cover are chromosomes. Chromosomes are the structures that collect and neatly hold together all the parts. Chromosomes collect the molecules and the chemicals that compose the genome and put them into an ordered form.

But the human genome is not a *single* book. In fact, it could be pictured as a set of encyclopedias. There are a total of 46 chromosomes in the human genome, or 46 encyclopedia volumes. These volumes have a curious characteristic: They are bound into pairs. There are two copies of the "A" volume paired together, two copies of the "B" volume paired together, and so on. This way, if there is a misprint in one of the volumes, there is a good chance that the other volume will have a clear entry. So the human genome actually has 23 *pairs* of chromosomes that add up to a total of 46.

Just as individual volumes of an encyclopedia deal with different subject matter, different chromosome pairs group together different types of information.

Instead of being organized in alphabetical order, the volumes of chromosomes are organized by related functions. Some chromosomes group together information that controls cell functions. Other chromosomes group together information that controls eye color, hair color, etc.

Entries in an encyclopedia are written on paper. In the genomic encyclopedia, the paper could be compared to molecules of DNA. Written on this "paper" are the "paragraphs" and the "words" that instruct life how to form and maintain itself. These paragraphs are the equivalent of genes.

Genes tell cells what to do. Just as paragraphs are a coherent collection of words, genes are a collection of codes that give meaning and direction to a cell. In a book, some paragraphs are long and some are short. In the genome, some collections of genes are made of long sequences, and some are made of short sequences. In a sense, genes are the words that tell all the parts of the body what to do.

Words are made of letters, just as genes are made of nucleotides. Like the letters of a word, the way in which the nucleotides are combined determines the meaning. The word "stand," for instance, has a specific meaning. But by subtracting one letter, a word with a completely different meaning appears. Subtract the "t" from "stand" and you have the word "sand." The two words are quite similar in spelling but worlds apart in meaning. The same holds true of nucleotides. Within nucleotide arrangements, the presence or absence of a single "letter" completely changes the meaning of the gene and, in turn, completely changes how a gene functions.

To review: The metaphorical book of the human genome consists of chromosomes, which act like a spine and outer cover to hold together all the parts. Chromosomes are structures that group similar types of information together. Genes are like paragraphs of words that give meaning to each section of the book. DNA is like the paper, giving the words a place to be. Finally, a word's letters are like the individual nucleotides that make up the basic parts of the genes.

# Inside the Genome

## CHAPTER TWO

How do all these parts—chromosomes, genes, and DNA—work together to support life? Like the very structure of the genome itself, the process is both simple and complex at the same time. Even as you sit reading this book, the cells of your body are at work. Some are dividing. Some are issuing commands to produce proteins. Some are dying. The inner workings of the body never stop during an organism's lifetime.

One of the most basic functions of genes is to create copies of themselves. Remember, each new cell receives a full set of your genome. The duplication of genetic material happens whenever a cell divides. Cell division takes place all the time inside the body. Dying and worn-out cells must be replaced. Sometimes a trauma, such as a cut or a bruise, will provide the signal for the body to create new cells. When a cell receives a signal to divide, it also receives a signal to make a copy of the genome inside it. The process that leads to cell division is called "mitosis." Mitosis is the method by which the genetic material in the nucleus of a cell duplicates itself in preparation for the cell to divide and create a new, identical copy. To understand how mitosis works, it's necessary to understand a little more about the structure of DNA.

DNA is a large molecule. In fact, it is called a "macromolecule," which means "exceptionally large molecule." DNA is actually a combination of many molecules. If all the DNA molecules in a single cell were unraveled and placed end-to-end, they would stretch nearly three feet (1 m) long. Thousands upon thousands of simple molecules combine together to make a single strand of DNA. With its molecules stacked together, the DNA strand takes on a shape called a "double helix," which is a gentle twist, like the twist of a spiral staircase.

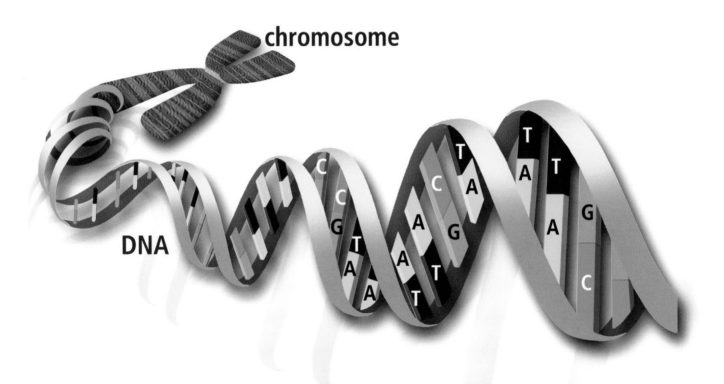

chromosome

DNA

There are four basic molecules, called "bases," that make up DNA: adenine, cytosine, guanine and thymine. They are usually referred to by their first letters: adenine is "A," cytosine is "C," guanine is "G," and thymine is "T."

A, C, T, and G display a curious feature. They are like the pieces of a puzzle. The A base will only combine with the T base, the way a puzzle piece will only fit with a piece that matches it. This also holds true for C and G. The C base combines only with the G base. Because of their specific molecular shape, it is impos-

**DNA is composed of four bases with specific attractions. "A" (adenine) will only bind with "T" (thymine). And "G" (guanine) will only bind with "C" (cytosine).**

sible to make matches any other way. If A tries to combine with G or C, the two parts bounce off one another.

The A-T base connection and the C-G base connection are called "base pairs." Base pairs are the simple building blocks of genes. Sequences of A-T and C-G base pairs can yield an almost endless number of combinations. These combinations are the codes, or instructions, that determine what a gene's function will be.

When a cell prepares to divide, the first thing that happens is that the tightly twisted DNA strands that make up the chromosomes begin to unravel. The base

Since "A" will only bind with "T," the DNA molecule is capable of splitting and making exact copies of itself every time a cell is ready to divide.

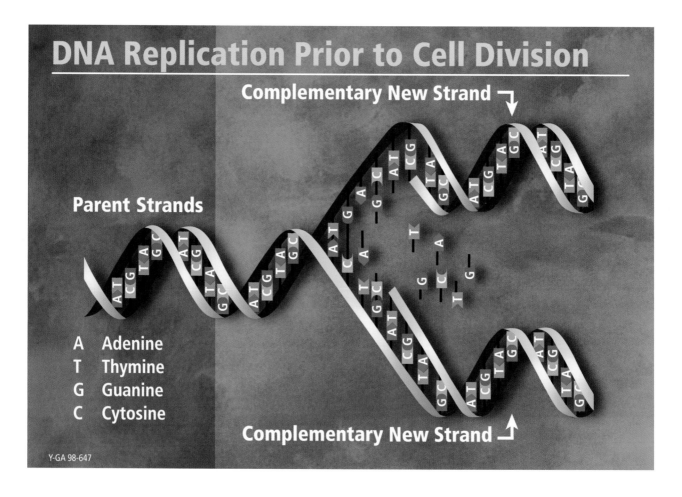

**DNA Replication Prior to Cell Division**

Complementary New Strand

Parent Strands

A    Adenine
T    Thymine
G    Guanine
C    Cytosine

Complementary New Strand

Y-GA 98-647

pairs are pulled apart, leaving them open and no longer joined to their complementary bases. The cell is now ready to make a complete copy of its genome.

Inside the cell, there are plenty of spare parts, composed of A, C, T, and G. As the DNA strand begins to unwind, it attracts to it the bases that fit naturally. So, for example, unwinding a single A-T base pair leaves two strands, one with an empty A socket, the other with an empty T socket. A special protein structure called an "enzyme" collects spare bases from within the cell and fits them to the empty bases. In this example, the enzyme, finding an empty A socket, fits a matching T to the DNA strand. On the other half of the strand, an empty T socket is fitted with its matching A base.

The strands of DNA unwrap and recombine very quickly. As soon as an empty base appears, a complementary base is fitted to it. Lagging a little behind this process is an enzyme that closes the exposed gene and twists it up into a compact mass again. Picture a coat with two zippers. As one zipper is pulled down, it opens the coat. Another zipper follows directly behind the first one, closing up the coat. When the entire chromosome is unraveled and matched with newly formed bases, the result is two full copies of the genome in one cell.

Now, with two copies of the entire genome existing within it, the single cell is ready to divide. The two copies move to opposite ends of the cell and the cell itself splits in half. Each half has a full copy of the genome. The ongoing process of mitosis continues within many cells at the same time, replacing cells that die, or in response to a body trauma where more cells are needed to repair damage.

A gene is not a single A-T or C-G connection. Rather, a gene is a long series of A-T and C-G connections. Sometimes thousands of these A-T / C-G connections are needed to make a single gene. Usually, there is a "dead space" between active genes composed of repeating A-T / C-G connections that do not code for any life processes. Special molecules signal the beginning of a new gene and its end. This makes each gene into a separate unit, and ensures that the codes of active genes are not confused with one another.

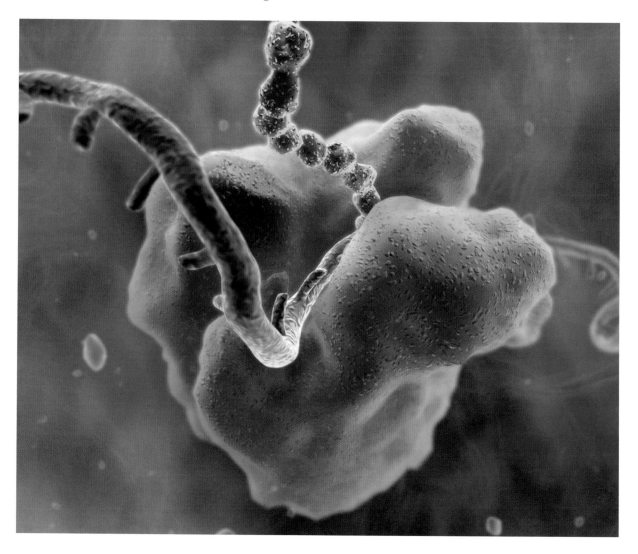

Ribosomes are found toward the outer edges of cells. This is an actual photomicrograph of a ribosome taken from a living cell. (The color has been added.)

An estimated 40,000 genes are present in the human genome. And yet, within a single cell, just one or two pairs of genes are active. This way, a cell knows to behave like a skin cell or a heart muscle cell or a brain nerve cell and ignore all the other codes contained in its genome. The genes themselves do not make anything, but they do set off a chain of events that shapes every cell in the human body and gives it its identity.

generated at different points of the DNA. When each piece is present, they bind, and new protein is created by the cell.

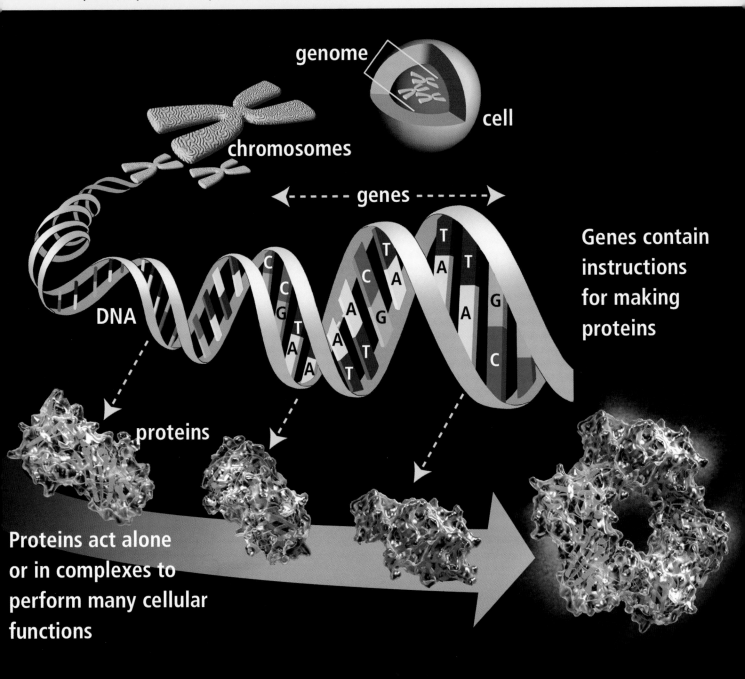

genome

cell

chromosomes

genes

DNA

C C
T A
A T
A

C
A T
G
T

T
A
A T
G
T
A G
C

Genes contain instructions for making proteins

proteins

Proteins act alone or in complexes to perform many cellular functions

In the human body there are specialized cells that carry only one-half the normal number of chromosomes. Scientists calls these cells haploids. In men, the sperm cell is a haploid. In women, the egg cell is a haploid. Sexual reproduction involves a mother and a father, both providing one-half of the genetic material that fuses together to make the unique genome of a new person.

When a gene in a cell is active, it is called an "expressed" gene. The codes and instructions imbedded in expressed genes tell the cell what to do. Genes are responsible for every single function in the body. The mechanism behind gene expression goes like this: A small segment of DNA unwinds from the chromosome and exposes itself inside the nucleus. This small area is the expressed gene. Its expressed state seems to send a signal out to the rest of the cell. Bits and pieces of molecular building blocks enter the nucleus and move toward the expressed gene. The exposed genetic code, the string of A-T/C-G sequences, attracts molecules that copy the code.

This is the chief function of an expressed gene: To expose its code and to allow it to be copied to molecules that act as messengers. These messenger molecules then make a journey out of the cell nucleus to a cellular structure called the "ribosome." Ribosomes are located near the outer edges of cells. The molecules enter the ribosome, transferring the message from the genes.

When the ribosome receives its message, it begins to work. The transferred instructions from the genes are precise instructions for making substances called "proteins." The ribosome manufactures the proteins according to the gene's instructions. The function of some proteins is to combine other molecules together. Proteins that combine other molecules together are called "enzymes." Once they are manufactured by the cell's ribosome, the proteins and enzymes begin *their* work.

Proteins perform nearly all the body's functions. Some proteins, for example, reduce large food molecules to tinier parts so the body can absorb and use food energy. Other proteins remove oxygen from the air you inhale and bind it to cells. Still other proteins act as enzymes and take bits of molecules and combine them into entirely new molecules that are needed for other purposes in the body.

Each cell in the human body is programmed to express certain genes and to ignore others. This way a liver cell, for instance, is given its role and function as a liver cell and not as a nerve cell or a blood cell. In order for the body to remain a collection of parts that operate together smoothly, each cell must be directed to express certain genes and to ignore others. If cells were not directed in this manner, no life would be possible. A fingernail or an eyeball suddenly appearing in the heart would spell disaster.

To review: Proteins control all essential aspects of a living organism. All chemical reactions that allow human life to take place can be traced back to commands issued by the expressed genes in your cells. When a specific set of genes are expressed, they issue commands to make a certain type of protein. These proteins, in turn, direct the functioning of all cells.

## Tracing Genetic Flaws

CHAPTER THREE

Diseases come from a variety of sources. Some are caused by bacteria. The body fights bacterial diseases by unleashing white blood cells and other antibodies. They seek out and destroy bacteria that have invaded the body. Viral diseases are different. A viral disease is caused by an organism that injects bits of its DNA into your cells. The cells become "hijacked," producing more cells that are enslaved to create copies of the virus. Generally, these types of diseases are also quickly controlled by the body's defensive systems.

A third type of disease is centered in the genes themselves. "Genetic diseases" are caused when a gene, or a gene group, is not correctly copied by the cell. Genetic diseases are usually inherited. If both mother and father harbor a gene that is

The anatomy of a typical virus is pictured here. The "spikes" enable the virus to cling to a living cell in a plant or animal. It injects its own DNA into the cell's nucleus and takes over command of the cell. It then uses the plant's or animal's cellular equipment to make proteins that are necessary for the virus to live. But the cells of the host will die.

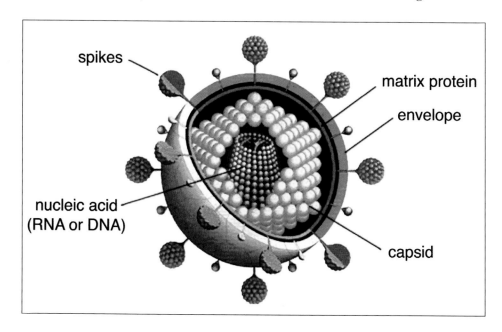

spikes

matrix protein

envelope

nucleic acid
(RNA or DNA)

capsid

flawed, the flawed gene can be passed on to their children. The flawed gene then becomes part of the child's genome and is copied and reproduced in the body.

Remember that the human genome is like a set of encyclopedias with two copies of each volume. If the genetic instructions on one of the volumes are flawed, the cell will "read" the other copy of the gene that is found in the duplicate volume. This kind of safeguard usually ensures that if a flawed copy of a gene is present, it will be overruled in favor of an unflawed copy. This system keeps genetic flaws from becoming commonplace.

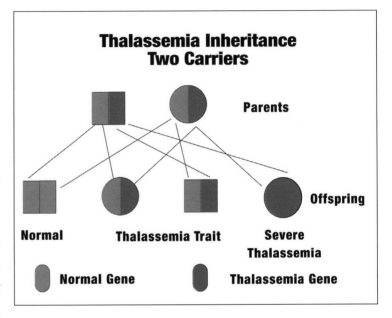

Most genetic diseases stem from a genome carrying two flawed copies of a gene. The end result is that the body fails to make the correct proteins that govern cell functions. Hemophilia, for example, is a genetic disease. In hemophiliacs, the protein that is responsible for blood clotting is not produced. As a result, the slightest bump can result in massive internal bleeding. A simple scratch or a bloody nose can be fatal.

Even small flaws in the gene sequence can be a disaster. Thalassemia is a condition where just one code out of sequence results in the absence of just one protein. This protein is hemoglobin, which carries oxygen to blood cells. Thalassemia

Both mother and father need to carry the recessive gene for the illness thalassemia in order to pass it along to their children. If both parents have it, of every four children they may have, one will be normal, one will be severely stricken with the disease, and the remaining two will carry the gene but not manifest the disease.

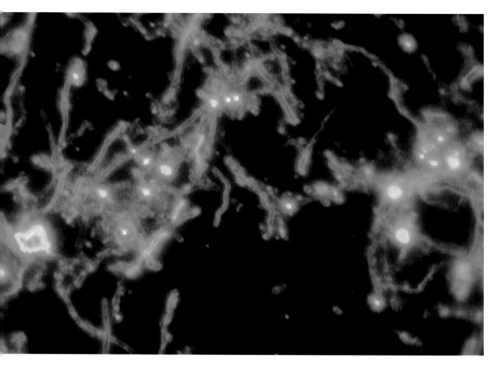

A photomicrograph of the bacteria *Actinomyces naeslundi*, which causes serious problems with a person's immune system. This sample has been stained with a fluorescent green liquid to make the bacteria easier to see under a microscope.

is a genetic disease that causes great pain, because the body suffers from not having enough oxygen.

The nature of the genome protects against many genetic flaws becoming commonplace by carrying genes that are both dominant (expressed) and recessive (not expressed). Flaws are nearly always recessive in nature. So if a person carries one copy of a flawed, recessive gene, and the other copy is dominant and unflawed, the dominant gene will be expressed. Even if a person carries the flawed gene for a genetic disease such as thalassemia, if the other, normal gene is present, it will dominate and hemoglobin will be produced. The genetic disease, in this case, fails to appear. The extra copy means that for someone to suffer from a genetic disorder, they must have a double dose of the recessive gene.

Genetic diseases are difficult to treat. In the near future, scientists hope to be able to treat genetic diseases in this fashion: First, the specific gene sequence that is out of whack must be identified. Then, the specific flaw must be determined. This might be done by comparing a copy of the normal gene with a copy of the flawed gene.

Once the flaw is determined, a new, corrected strand of gene code must be made. But the tricky part is getting this new code into the cells, and getting it to multiply and grow. Scientists think viruses have the potential to single out cells and deliver to them new genetic coding. In nature, this is what viruses do: Seek out cells and inject a strand of their own genetic code into the cell nucleus. If the harmful genetic code inside many viruses were removed, and a genetic code carrying a corrected gene sequence inserted, it could be a means of "infecting" the cell with a genetic code that corrects a genetic disorder.

Recently, this type of treatment has been used to help children with "bubble boy disease," a genetic illness brought on by the body failing to produce the disease-battling white blood cells necessary to defend against harmful bacteria. A virus with a corrected code was introduced to the children and began to produce the genetic code necessary for making white blood cells. Unfortunately, the treatment had a harmful side effect. The children developed leukemia, which is an overabundance of white blood cells. So it would seem that the treatment of genetic diseases still needs more study to be effective.

## DNA Profiling

Only identical twins have identical DNA. For everyone else, a person's DNA is like a fingerprint, unique to one person in the world. Police use this trait to identify criminals and victims in a process called "DNA profiling." DNA profiling requires only a small amount of cells—a bit of bone, some skin, or even a person's dried saliva from the back of a stamp.

Scientists start by bursting the cells to free the DNA. Then they add a protein that makes lots of copies of the DNA to make a larger sample. Most DNA looks the same, but there are about seven short areas on DNA that are unique to each person. Scientists photograph these areas and compare them with the same areas on samples to find a match.

Samples taken from a crime scene can place a criminal at the location. In the case of a missing person, found samples can be matched to skin cell samples from clothing or even hair follicles from a brush.

# The Two Faces of Mutation

CHAPTER FOUR

There are times when a genetic flaw is copied over and over again and passed along through many generations of people. Such flaws then become a normal part of the population. One example of a flaw becoming a normal part of a population can be found in some people of African descent. After thousands of years of battling malaria, some Africans have developed resistance to this disease. The blood cells of people who are naturally resistant to malaria are not shaped like donuts, as they are in most people. Instead, they are shaped like a crescent, or a sickle. Blood cells like this resist the invasion of malaria. But there is a trade-off for the resistance. These malaria-resistant sickle cells tend to stick and collect in smaller blood vessels, causing sharp pain and an illness called "sickle cell anemia."

**This photomicrograph shows red blood cells that have been deformed by sickle-cell anemia.**

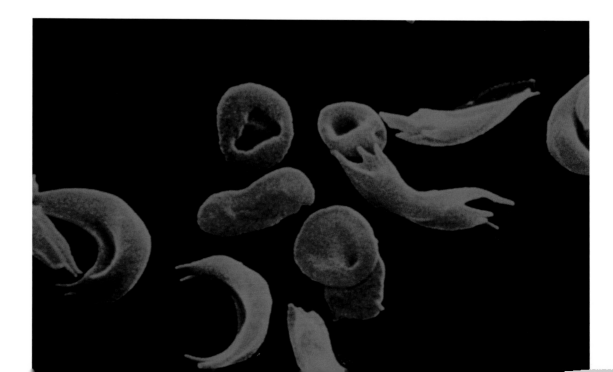

Most people associate mutations with diseases and disorders. But in nature, mutations can sometimes play a key role in survival. One example of a mutation in the human genome that is helpful can be traced to people who lived for thousands of years in northern climates, such as northern Europe and Mongolia. All babies can digest milk, but as people grow older, the gene that produces the protein that allows milk to be digested is turned off. Yet in some populations, sometime in the distant past, the ability for adults to digest milk became essential for survival. So, through mutation, the milk-digesting gene remained active throughout a person's lifetime. This mutated gene, in turn, was passed along to children.

Even today, many adults have trouble digesting milk. And yet, there are also plenty of adults who have no trouble digesting milk. The mutation that allows some adults to drink a quart of milk without getting sick has been passed down and still exists today. The presence of this mutation, sometime in the distant past, increased the chances of survival. Because it was useful, it continued to be passed down through the generations.

Some scientists believe that the racial differences that characterize the family of man can be traced to mutations that helped different populations survive in different environments. The lighter skin tones and fair hair of many northern Europeans may have been such a mutation. In these colder northern climates, there is much less sunlight during the course of a year. Fairer skin would have absorbed more sunlight than darker skin. Sunlight triggers the production of vitamin D in the body when its ultraviolet rays excite fat cells in the skin. Without ample vitamin D, the body suffers from weak bones because it cannot absorb calcium. This condition is called rickets and results in limbs that are bent and bowed.

Some scientists think that in the cloudy, harsh climate of prehistoric Europe, fair-skinned people had a survival advantage by having skin that was more sensitive to sunlight, and more easily triggered the production of vitamin D. Scientists believe that this mutation may have favored the survival of fair-skinned people in prehistoric Europe.

On the other side of the coin, the tropics are usually characterized by powerful sunlight. Dark-skinned people produce more melanin, a pigment produced by the body to protect it from the harmful overexposure to sunlight. Some scientists believe that this trait—dark skin with plenty of melanin—gave people a survival advantage in sunny, hot climates by blocking the entry of too much solar radiation.

To use another example, the curly hair of many Africans allows air to flow near the

Top: Most mutations are not beneficial, and those animals born with severe mutations usually do not live long. Two-headed snakes do not usually survive to adulthood in the wild.

Bottom: Some mutations, however, may be beneficial to both the individual animal and its entire species. The lighter-colored peppered moth has less natural camouflage while on the bark of its favorite tree than does the peppered moth that has a mutation for darker coloring.

Some genes are called "recessive genes" while others are called "dominant genes." Dominant genes always win in a war of genetic expression. With the exceptions of red blood cells and cells related to reproduction, each human cell has 46 chromosomes paired into 23 sets in its nucleus. This means there are two sets of DNA coding for the same function. If two genes code for the same trait, the dominant trait will be expressed in that person. If one gene for a specific trait is dominant and the other is recessive, the dominant still wins. Only when two copies of a recessive trait appear on the genes is a recessive trait expressed. Recessive traits in people include blue eyes and red hair. Genetic diseases such as hemophilia and Down syndrome are also recessive traits.

skull, which helps keep a person cool. Straight, thick hair found on many people who live in northern Europe is excellent at insulating the top of the head to keep it from losing heat. So, environmental pressures can play a role in making mutations a common feature in certain populations.

Animals, too, rely on mutations to help them better fit into their environments. As established animal populations begin to expand into new areas, slight changes in their species may help them better adapt to their new environments. So, for example, if a white moth population begins to expand into a forest of black trees, it may be easily spotted and eaten by predators. Slight mutations that produce a gray moth or even a black moth might give these insects a better chance of survival. Charles Darwin called this "natural selection." If two animals have slightly different attributes, the one whose attributes contribute better to its survival will be more likely to survive. That means it is more likely to pass along its slightly different genes. And this means that the slightly different animal will become the norm for that species. Darwin described it as nature selecting the animals better suited for survival over the others.

# CHAPTER FIVE

Apples tend to reproduce like people. That is, apple seeds are similar to, but not identical with, the fruit of the trees from which they come. This means that in the wild, every generation of apples will taste slightly different. And after several generations, the fruit will not taste at all like that of the original tree. So in order to make all apple trees bear fruit that always looks and tastes the same, the trees must be cloned.

Nearly every cell in the human body carries a complete copy of the human genome. When cells go through the process of mitosis and divide, the cells are "cloning" themselves. They are producing new versions of themselves that contain genetic material that is *identical* to its source. That is the definition of a clone.

This has led to the theory that just a single cell, with its entire copy of an individual's genome inside it, could be used to create a whole person. The process is called cloning, and the identical new person is called a clone, since he or she would have a genome identical to the original. In theory, the idea should work. But the science of cloning still has major scientific hurdles to cross before cloning a person or an animal from just a single cell becomes commonplace.

Cloning has been sometimes misunderstood as a radical new technology. But in many plants and in some animals, cloning is a common method of reproduction. One example of a plant that reproduces by cloning is the spider plant, common to many homes and offices. The spider plant sends out new shoots, or "baby spiders," from the parent plant that look like miniature versions of the big plant. If you clip off the babies and allow them to root, you have a new plant. This new plant is a clone. Its genetic material is identical to the genetic material of the adult.

Many fruits and vegetables purchased at markets are also clones. This way, the Macintosh apples you ate last year taste the same as the Macintosh apple you might eat today. This type of cloning is a little different from the way spider plants clone themselves. In the case of cloning Macintosh apple trees, branches from an older, fully grown Macintosh apple tree are grafted onto a partially grown apple tree. A V-shaped cut is made across the trunk of the young apple tree. A branch from the tree that produced the best apples is then placed in the notch and bound to the new tree. This is called grafting. When the graft takes, the tree will produce fruit that is identical to the fruit that was produced by the old tree.

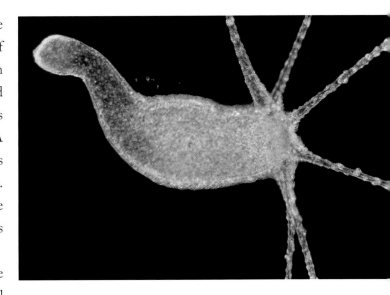

The hydra is a simple, multi-celled aquatic organism that reproduces via cloning. The tentacles at its top have stinging cells at their ends that allow the hydra to capture and paralyze its prey.

Some simpler forms of animal life also reproduce by cloning. The hydra, an almost microscopic animal that lives in fresh water, is an example of an animal that reproduces by cloning. When it is ready to reproduce, the hydra sends a bud from its body that forms into a branch shape. This branch falls off and eventually becomes a new creature. The genetic material of the parent and its offspring are identical, making it a clone.

Although cloning is common in nature and is natural in many plants and animals, it becomes an adventure in science when attempts are made to clone organisms that, by nature, do *not* reproduce by cloning.

Again, the process of cloning an animal is simple—in theory. If you want to clone a sheep, the first thing needed is a fertilized egg cell from a sheep. This egg cell is then removed from the mother. Next, the genetic material in the nucleus of the fertilized egg cell is removed. It is replaced with the chromosomes of the sheep that is to be cloned. The altered egg cell is returned to the mother's womb. The egg then follows its natural function, dividing and growing, following the blueprint inside of it. The sheep is pregnant and gives birth to a new sheep. But instead of having DNA that was supplied by the mother, the sheep has DNA that was inserted by the scientist.

"Dolly" the sheep became a world-famous clone in 1996. She was cloned by the use of this technique. Scientists in Scotland started by removing a newly fertilized egg cell from a female sheep. The nucleus was removed from the fertilized egg and replaced with chromosomes from the animal to be cloned. The modified egg was returned to the mother's womb. Later, she gave birth to Dolly, an animal that shared no genes with her mother but was a genetically identical copy of an unrelated adult sheep.

But at age six, about half the life span of an ordinary sheep, Dolly began to get sick. The first sign that something was wrong was when Dolly began to gain so much weight that she became obese. Shortly after this development, she was found to have arthritis. This disease causes a wearing down of the protective material between bones at the joints. Losing this material results in the bones grinding against each other as an animal moves, which can be extremely painful. Dolly became increasingly sick and was then found to have lung cancer. Arthritis and lung cancer are common when sheep reach about 11 or 12 years of age. It seemed that the aging process in Dolly was speeded up. To keep the animal from suffering, she was put to sleep.

No one is sure if Dolly's illness and death was the result of her being a clone. But her death ignited a storm of debate in scientific circles. Some say Dolly's illness is unconnected to her being a clone. Others say the premature aging of Dolly is a warning that cloning larger animals is bound to fail.

Still, work goes on in cloning animals. Today, mice are regularly cloned through the technique described above, providing identical lab subjects for researchers around the world. Some livestock have also been cloned, but at pres-

This lamb is Dolly (left), the first cloned sheep, with her surrogate mother.

ent, cloned livestock are not as common as cloned mice. One of the benefits of cloned livestock is that once farmers find the individual animal that produces the most meat or the best milk, an exact copy of that animal can be cloned and copied. This results in a predictable yield from the animals that livestock growers can rely on. Cloned livestock may become common in the near future.

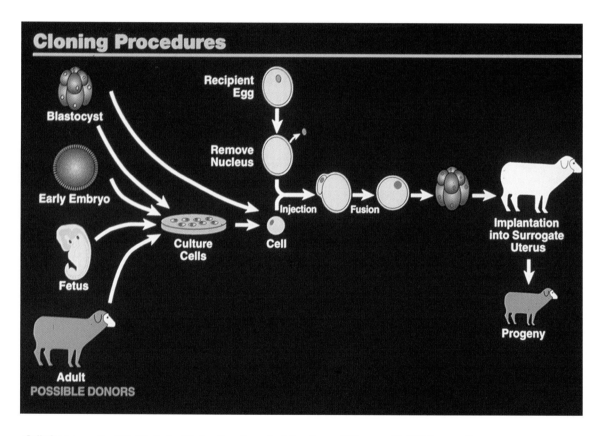

Cells from an animal that is desired to be cloned may be taken from a "blastocyst," which is an embryo that has developed for five to seven days. Or they may be taken from an early embryo, a fetus, or even from an adult animal. The cells are "cultured," or grown in a laboratory. The egg from an animal in which the clone is to be grown has its nucleus removed; the genetic material from the cultured cells is injected to replace it. The egg is then implanted into the surrogate mother. It will now develop according to the genetic instructions from the injected cellular material and not that of the surrogate mother.

But some scientists envision another way to use cloning techniques. Endangered animals may benefit from advances in the new science. Some animals that are endangered are genetically similar to animals that are not endangered. One example is the "gaur," a cowlike animal that lives in Africa and Southeast Asia. If the genetic material of a gaur could be implanted in the fertilized egg of a cow, it's possible that a cow could give birth to a gaur.

Using cloning in this way could help reestablish endangered animal populations. It is also possible that completely extinct animals could be brought back to life with cloning. Mammoths, extinct for some 10,000 years, share many genetic similarities with elephants. If a good copy of the complete mammoth genome could be found, it is possible that it could be introduced into an elephant's fertilized egg. A mammoth is a good candidate for the first extinct animal to be brought back to life.

Cloning is one way to make identical copies of either a plant or an animal. But cells can be cloned, too. As mentioned previously, the process of mitosis is an act of cloning, since the cell divides and both cells end up with an exact copy of the genetic material. But scientists would like to be able to clone a very special cell produced by the body called a "stem cell."

Cells divide to produce new copies. But at times, the body needs more raw materials to grow or to repair itself than cell division alone can provide. In such a case, the body makes a remarkable cell called the stem cell. Stem cells carry the entire genome, like most cells in the body do. But the gene sequence that instructs a cell to be a hair or a tongue cell or a kidney cell is not yet active. Stem cells are like blank cells that can be programmed to be anything in the body.

Embryos inside the mother's womb produce the most stem cells. This makes sense because in just nine months, a single cell divides and grows to become a fully formed human being. And up until the age of about 18, stem cells are produced in abun-

It is possible that some endangered species may be saved by cloning, such as this African gaur.

dance in the human body. They provide the raw material that constructs growing bones, muscles, and organs. Stem cells rise from the core of bones, from an area called the marrow. They flow into the blood stream and are carried to different parts of the body where they are needed. When they arrive, they are modified by proteins to become whatever the body needs them to be. The brain also produces stem cells, but these are only used to replace dead or damaged cells in the brain.

Knowing the programmable nature of stem cells has led science to an interesting idea. In theory, stem cells could be cloned and programmed to become any part of the human body. Someone suffering from heart disease, for example, might be able to receive injections of stem cells and actually regenerate a new, healthy heart. The study and use of stem cells could lead to a whole new branch of medical treatment.

Unfortunately, stem cells are not easy to come by. Cloning stem cells tends to make them randomly develop into specific types of body cells rather than the "blank slates" scientists want to find. The most common source of stem cells for research purposes is the umbilical material of aborted fetuses. This has brought up many moral questions that have restricted the study of stem cells in the United States. However, new research suggests that stem cells may also be available from the placental tissue of normally born, healthy babies, as well as from the bone marrow of healthy adults.

If scientists could develop a reliable way to clone stem cells it would open up a whole new avenue for treating diseases that destroy internal organs. New, healthy organs might be grown in laboratories and made available for people whose own organs have become diseased or have ceased to function.

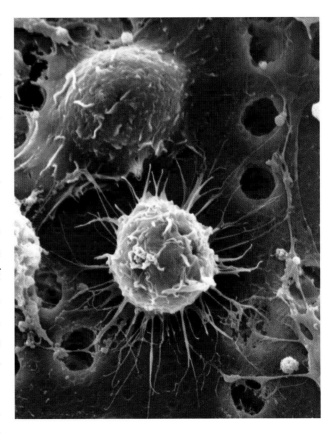

**Above:** A photomicrograph of a human stem cell, the miraculous cell that is capable of becoming any part of the body—from blood to bone to brain.

**Opposite:** Much has been made of the possibility of cloning a mammoth, such as the one pictured here. But first, enough genetic material must be found to reconstruct the entire mammoth genome.

## Genetic Engineering

CHAPTER SIX

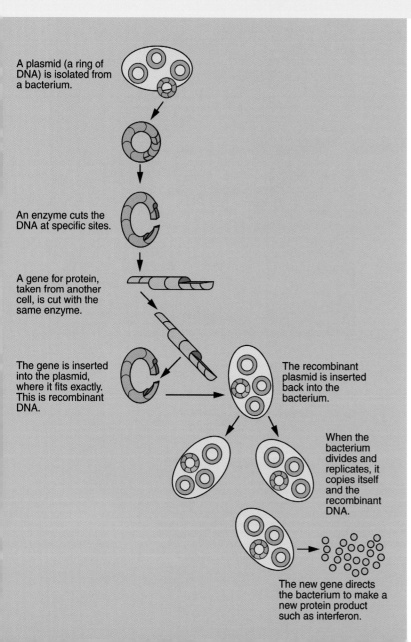

A plasmid (a ring of DNA) is isolated from a bacterium.

An enzyme cuts the DNA at specific sites.

A gene for protein, taken from another cell, is cut with the same enzyme.

The gene is inserted into the plasmid, where it fits exactly. This is recombinant DNA.

The recombinant plasmid is inserted back into the bacterium.

When the bacterium divides and replicates, it copies itself and the recombinant DNA.

The new gene directs the bacterium to make a new protein product such as interferon.

The exploration of the human genome has led to some fantastic advances for science. Remember that chromosomes are made largely of DNA, and that DNA holds genes in place. Genes in turn issue the orders for making proteins, and proteins control the chemical and physical processes that allow life to exist.

The study of genetic material has allowed scientists to pinpoint specific proteins that are involved in the processes that allow genes to be expressed. Researchers have also identified the protein that actually snips sections of DNA from its strand, and a protein that recombines sections of DNA with the original strand. They have harnessed these proteins and can use them in a process called "gene splicing."

This gene splicing technique is also

This sequence shows how geneticists are using bacteria to manufacture needed human proteins such as interferon, which is used to treat such serious diseases as hepatitis. This process is called gene splicing.

Like a genie in a bottle, **DNA** holds the potential for fulfilling many human dreams, from curing chronic and childhood diseases to genetically engineering food plants and animals. As we continue to unravel its secrets, more and more possibilities will become available.

Giantism and dwarfism are genetic diseases. The woman shown here is of normal size.

A close-up of *E. coli* bacteria, which can cause severe stomach and gastrointestinal problems. Now, genetic scientists are using this harmful bug to produce helpful human proteins.

known as "recombinant DNA." Currently, it is used extensively in a well-known bacterium called *E. coli*. This microscopic animal contains rings of genetic instructions in tiny, internal structures called "plasmids." A plasmid ring is removed and a protein used to snip open the genetic codes. New genes are added and another protein seals the plasmid ring. Then, the genetically modified structure is returned to the bacterium.

The result is a genetically engineered bacterium with a new gene added. When a human gene is added to *E. coli* bacteria, the results can be impressive. Guided by the human gene added to its plasmid ring, *E. coli* turns into a living factory that will produce human proteins. In medicine, some of these proteins are critical for certain medical treatments. By inserting the human genes that produce insulin into *E. coli*, vast amounts of insulin can be manufactured. Insulin controls the amount of sugar in the bloodstream and is critical to the health of diabetics. The genes that control human growth hormone have been identified, and when spliced into the plasmid rings of *E. coli*, the bacteria produce human growth hormone, which is used to treat people with dwarfism.

Genetic engineering through gene splicing has opened up new possibilities for medical treatments. One of the most interesting developments is the creation of animals that include the genes of human beings in their genomes.

# Mixing and Matching Genes

CHAPTER SEVEN

Recombinant DNA techniques are used to produce a living animal that expresses human genes. These creatures are called "transgenic animals." For years, medical researchers have used the organs of certain animals to replace damaged human organs. But the human body often rejects animal organ transplants because it recognizes the organ as foreign.

Transgenic animals are created by scientists using a combination of cloning and gene splicing techniques. As in cloning, a fertilized egg is removed from the animal. The genetic material is extracted. What is inserted is genetic material that has been modified by scientists. In the case of transgenic animals, the animal's ordinary genome has been spliced with human genes. The idea is that if the animal's genome includes genes that are common to humans, then its transplanted organs are less likely to be rejected by the human body.

Most transgenic animals are pigs, whose organs or parts of organs are used to save human lives. There is a lot of controversy involved with transgenic animals. Some people protest that the animals are being treated cruelly. Some people in the scientific community worry that transgenic animals will create a bridge for diseases that afflict pigs to cross over between species and suddenly appear in humans. Still others worry about the idea that human beings are distorting nature.

These kinds of questions spark intense debate in scientific and political circles. But the fact remains that many, many people would not be alive today if not for the organs and body parts of transgenic animals.

The human genome is a complex set of genes that gives rise to human form and governs the chemistry and physical reality of human beings. In 2002, a complete map of the human genome was produced that identified about 40,000 gene sequences. But we have only a dim idea of what the map means. We have identified the areas where sequences of genes are active in producing the biochemical processes that power life. But we do not know what most of these genes produce, or how the proteins whose creation they prompt function in the human body.

Years of research may be needed before we have even a basic understanding of the map our science has produced. The time and resources needed for this job could be huge. But the benefits would be huge, too. Being able to reverse certain genetic disorders, or to cure all forms of cancer, or to prompt sight in someone who has been blind since birth, are just a few. Understanding the map of the human genome and being able to manipulate it could increase the quality of all human life.

This transgenic mouse has been given green, luminescent cells taken from a jellyfish through gene-splicing. It is one of 80 such mice that have been cloned. Some scientists think that by making certain cells luminescent it will help with cellular implantation in patients needing the procedure.

## Looking to the Future

CHAPTER EIGHT

The movie *Jurassic Park* fired the imagination of the world by suggesting that dinosaurs may someday be brought back to life through cloning. But there are many problems with the dream of cloning dinosaurs. In almost all cases, the remains of dinosaurs are fossils. Rock has taken the place of the living tissue, and there is no genetic material to recover. In the few cases of excavated dinosaurs that have been mummified, the genetic material in their cells has broken up and become random pieces, so the genome has been lost. The further back in time the animal existed, the less likely it is to be successfully cloned. And even if the genome of a dinosaur was discovered intact, what living animal could give birth

**Perhaps a reptile could give birth to a dinosaur egg, but judging from the size of it, a bird could not.**

to a dinosaur? The closest relatives to dinosaurs seem to be birds, and it is unlikely that a bird could give birth to a dinosaur egg.

In *Jurassic Park*, the problem of finding dinosaur DNA is cleverly solved by recovering it from the dried-up blood found in ancient insects that were encased in amber. If a mosquito bit a dinosaur, drank some of its blood, and then died, it *might* be possible to recover some dinosaur DNA from it. As to a host animal for birthing the dino clone, the film suggested that reptiles could be used. Of course, it is also shown in the movie that the scientists have miscalculated, and things go horribly wrong.

The sciences of genetic engineering and cloning clearly frighten some people—even some scientists. Should science be playing with the elements that direct the creation of life on Earth? People worry that if the secrets to these processes are known, they could be used in harmful ways. Perhaps genetic engineering could produce monsters. Perhaps black-hearted scientists would make a whole race of people who do nothing but work as slaves, while a small number of elite people enjoy the fruits of this labor. Perhaps, even worse, a genetically engineered virus could be created that destroys all human life.

But if we let our fears guide us, there would be no science. No one would invent anything for fear of what it might become. Science by its nature is an extension of the natural creativity found in all people. It is a curiosity that asks questions. It is a desire to know the how and why of the world, its animals and plants, and ourselves.

Genetic engineering and cloning must be used responsibly. Experiments must include a careful consideration of their outcomes, because these two branches of science have the potential to extend the reaches of humankind in ways that we can scarcely imagine at present. If used responsibly, genetic engineering could result in a future of health, peace, and prosperity for everyone on the planet.

**Opposite page: The movie *Jurassic Park*, and its sequels, had everyone thinking that cloning dinosaurs was just a few years away. But even with advanced technology, it will be virtually impossible. However, new, never-imagined-before animals are possible through cloning. Whether or not science should create them is a matter for serious discussion.**

# G L O S S A R Y

**antibodies** Substances produced by the body, such as white blood cells, to fight illness.

**arthritis** Inflammation of body joints.

**atoms of inheritance** Gregor Mendel's name for genes.

**base pairs** The two sets of molecules that make up DNA: adenine-thymine and cytosine-guanine.

**chromosome** Tiny structure inside the nucleus of a cell that carries DNA.

**cloning** The process of producing a new individual genetically identical to an existing individual.

**DNA** The chemical substance deoxyribonucleic acid, which carries the set of operating instructions for a living organism.

**dominant gene** A gene that is active in a cell and expresses a specific characteristic.

**double helix** The two-stranded spiral shape of DNA.

**Down syndrome** A genetic disease that is caused by two copies of a recessive trait appearing on the genome of an individual.

**enzymes** Special, complex protein structures.

**gaur** A large, wild ox found in Southeast Asia and Africa.

**gene** Element of an organism that contains hereditary information about a specific quality or trait.

**gene splicing** Process by which one DNA molecule or fragment can be attached to another.

**genetic engineering** Process of altering an animal or plant to ensure desired outcomes by manipulating its genome.

**genome** One set of chromosomes containing the entire genetic make-up of a species.

**grafting** Propagating better products by means of inserting a branch or tissue with desired qualities into a stock plant.

**haploid** Having half the normal number of chromosomes.

**hemoglobin** Protein in the blood that carries oxygen to cells.

**hemophilia** Genetic disease characterized by the lack of the blood-clotting protein.

**human genome** The blueprint that defines and maintains human traits and instructs cells how to develop.

**hydra** Very small, tube-shaped animal that lives in fresh water.

**leukemia** Acute or chronic disease characterized by overabundance of white blood cells.

**macromolecule** A very large molecule; usually a combination of several molecules.

**malaria** Disease caused by a parasite and transmitted by the bite of a mosquito.

**melanin** Dark animal or plant pigment.

**mitochrondrial DNA** A second set of DNA that is found outside the cell nucleus. It is made up of ring-shaped packages with 13 active genes and directs several critical life processes.

**mitosis** The process that leads to cell division.

**mutations** Significant alterations of, or relatively permanent changes to, hereditary material.

**natural selection** Slight changes or mutations in a species that may provide a better chance for the survival of that species.

**nucleotides** Specific sequences of molecules.

**recessive gene** Gene that is not active in a cell and is therefore not expressed.

**recombinant DNA** Result of gene-splicing technique where DNA is rejoined to its original strand using specific proteins.

**ribosome** Cellular structure where protein synthesis takes place.

**selective breeding** The development over time of plants and animals with desired qualities by keeping and breeding those that show the preferred qualities.

**sickle cell anemia** Hereditary condition resulting from a genetic mutation—development of blood cells shaped like crescents rather than donuts—that made some Africans resistant to malaria. These malaria resistant cells, however, tend to stick together in the smaller blood vessels, causing severe pain.

**stem cell** A cell with the full genome but with no gene sequence activated.

**thalassemia** Genetic disease in which the body lacks hemoglobin protein.

**transgenic animals** Animals that possess expressed human genes.